Transformation: The Process of Change

Stan E. DeKoven, Ph.D.

Transformation: The Process of Change

Stan E. DeKoven, Ph.D.

Copyright © 2016 by Stan DeKoven

ISBN 978-1-61529-172-4

Vision Publishing
1115 D Street
Ramona, CA 92065
1 800 9 VISION

www.booksbyvision.com

Table of Contents

Author's Foreword 5

Chapter 1 The Process of Change: Why is it so hard? 9

Chapter 2 Metamorphosis, Metanoia and Telios 13

Chapter 3 Transformation: Change My heart, change my wife,
and change my life 23

Chapter 4 Transforming My Church 29

Chapter 5 Living Stones 37

Chapter 6 Transformation of the World 41

Author's Foreword

Fontana Christian Fellowship International Ministries (FCFIM), pastored by Gary, Gina and now Kalina Holley, is growing. It did not grow for some time, not due to neglect, sin or circumstances, although Pastor Gina's health challenges did not help. But the church is growing, and getting stronger.

I have observed over the past few years that the church, like many faithful congregations, has gone through many changes…as we all do as people. Though some megachurches seemed to be expanding, and Christian T.V. continues to hype its influence, not much seemed to be happening with small to medium sized churches and ministries, but that seems to be changing (and did I mention that FCFIM is growing)?

The growth or transformation in FCFIM seems to be similar to other churches, and cannot be attributed to new programs, luck, chance or even strategies. It seems to be primarily due to a mixture of subtle changes, faithfulness and a fresh wind of the Holy Spirit, with the primary emphasis on faithfulness, where the church and its leadership has shown continued dedication to know Christ and make him known in the often troublesome city of Fontana, CA.

As you might imagine, I am honored to make my small contribution to the life of this growing New Testament church. It has been and continues to be a church willing to change, with focused ministry on helping people and their families make necessary changes to help them live the abundant life promised by Jesus. I admire the work being done here, for it is working, not in theory, but in reality.

My focus of teaching for the year 2014 was transformation; preparing for change. I am writing this book as a bit of a retrospective, as now we are in 2016, and change is working its way out in the hearts of God's people, and growth has come. The growth is not a direct result of the teaching, as the seeds of change have been sown by faithful leaders and other guest ministers in FCFIM for years, but the principles of transformation presented here may indeed accelerate the process of change which may lead to growth in the Kingdom of God for the reader, his or her family, and the church we so want to see grow.

Dr. Stan DeKoven

"Scared and sacred are spelled with the same letters. Awful proceeds from the same root word as awesome. Terrify and terrific. Every negative experience holds the seed of transformation."

— Alan Cohen

Chapter 1

The Process of Change:
Why is it so hard?

Reconciliation is the message of an exchanged life. Transformation is but the outworking of what Christ has already accomplished for us through his death, burial, resurrection and ascension to the throne…and of course, we are seated with him, far above all created things. We must, if we are going to discuss change or transformation, recognize that as believers we do not start from zero, but from the finished work of Christ which makes us already whole, complete, perfect (mature), and fully capable of fulfilling our divine destiny.

At the same time, all of us sin (which does not make us sinners, as in our primary and present condition, for we are no longer sinners but saints), and fall short of the ultimate glory of God, but we are forgiven, loved, precious, reconciled, and on we can go. At the same time, though perfect as new born babies from the moment God apprehends us by faith, there is a lot of growing, requiring changing, left to do. We call that maturation, becoming…but again, we start with every advantage, as we are created in God's image with purpose, and have been redeemed by his precious blood. Please never forget your launching point. It is the key to your transformation.

The fact is, change is not easy for any of us. Whether we think of change as individual or corporate, such as for a nation or church, it takes considerable effort, but change is indeed possible. In every way, we can trust that, due to the wonderful grace of God and the Spirit's work in our life, we are being conformed to his image. At the same time, scripture, which will be presented below, seems to indicate that change is up to us. Certainly, both are true, and will be thoroughly explored in this book.

For most of us, we recognize that change is inevitable (along with death and taxes), but without doubt, it appears to take so very long to change, and it is so painful. I have faced and dealt with a number of issues in my life, and can say with great joy that the victories I have achieved were not without effort, struggle, and help...but victory, already provided for us by Christ death and resurrection, can become our daily reality as we submit to the legitimate and grace filled process of change.

It Takes So Long: Three Brief Examples

Moses

As we should surely know, Moses had quite a journey before achieving his life purpose. The early part of his life, after his miraculous rescue, Moses was raised in the University of Egypt (Pharaohs' house) until his debacle in killing the Egyptian at age 40. For the next 40 years, Moses lived in the desert, learning the ways of the wilderness, in preparation for his leadership of the children of Israel. It took Moses nearly 80 years to be fully prepared to fulfill his destiny...and God knows just how long it will take for us to reach our maturity.

Jesus

Our Lord had every advantage. He was born in a loving family, was protected by angels and The Holy Spirit, and never suffered from the onslaught of T.V or the Internet. Being born without sin didn't hurt either. Even so, Jesus had to grow.

In Luke, Chapter 2:52, the bible says that Jesus grew in wisdom and knowledge, and in favor with God and man. If Jesus had to grow, transitioning through the natural changes of life, how much more do we?

Paul

According to Paul's own confession, he was raised in a wonderful family system, the best of all, he was a Benjamite. In time he became a religious leader (Pharisee) and zealous for the word and worship of God. Of course, his zeal was misdirected, but after encountering Christ on the road to Damascus, his zeal and training was properly directed to the expansion of the Kingdom of God. Yet, as well trained and passionate as Paul was, he also needed time for seasoning, serving in the wilderness for upwards of 14 years, and then tutelage under Barnabas before being launched into Missions ministry.

All of God's people (and there are no small people in God's kingdom) must mature, to achieve the wonderful purposes assigned by the Spirit as a full time member of God's eternal family.

It is important to remember, the goal is not perfection, but…maturity, and there are three biblical words that speak to this concept of maturity. They are Metamorphosis, Metanoia and Telios.

Chapter 2

Metamorphosis, Metanoia and Telios

The three words discussed here are important in our understanding of God's purposes for our transformation. All three are Greek words; their definitions with illustrations to follow help us in our journey.

Metamorphosis

Metamorphosis is defined by example as in an insect or amphibian; the process of transformation from an immature form to an adult form in two or more distinct stages. A change of the form or nature of a thing or person into a completely different one, by natural or supernatural means.

Metamorphosis is the word used to describe Jesus transformation on the mount of transfiguration, where he was "changed" (Matthew 17:2). Jesus' outer transformation was due to the outworking of his inner nature, or Deity, and he shined forth like the sun. Also, Christians are said to be in the process of being transformed (metamorphosis) by the Spirit of God (2 Corinthians 3:18). 2 Peter 3:18, expanded from the Greek states, "Grow (metamorphosis) in the sphere of grace and into the full knowledge of our Lord and Savior Jesus Christ". As we grow, we find that we are abler to live above the "old nature" and are "transformed by the renewing of our mind" into what God wants us to be, as our "new nature" shines through. Paul's oft quoted verse on the topic is from Roman's 12: 1-2, where we are urged to renew our minds through the Word of God.

If you will, for the believer metamorphosis is natural. It is supernaturally natural in that in the Holy Spirit, we become more like Jesus. Thus, we are urged to cooperate with the process, by submission to God the Word (Jesus) and the word of God. To change is a process, where God works in us and we work as well. It is a mutual process, an important one, and a joyful one.

Metanoia

When I was young I heard many messages regarding my need to repent to gain God's love and favor. Now I believe in repentance; when understood properly. My early understanding was repentance required weeping, wailing and gnashing of teeth (which is hell really); self-flagellation would help. The fact is, we need to change our thinking, as none of us have our minds fully lined up with God's word. Changing our thinking is key to our growth.

The noun metanoia, is translated "repentance in the King James" and its cognate verb metanoeō is translated "repent". Tertullian protested the unsuitable translation of the Greek metanoeo into the Latin paenitentiam agite by arguing that "in Greek, metanoia is not a confession of sins but a change of mind." "Conversion" (from the Latin conversiōn-em turning round) with its "change in character" meaning is more nearly the equivalent of metanoia than repentance. Synonyms for "conversion" include "change of heart" and "metanoia."

More than just confession, which is often void of true acceptance of responsibility for sin, metanoia speaks of changing our thinking that leads to fruitfulness, or a visible change in attitude and action.

Telios

Strong's Concordance defines Telios as having reached its end, i.e. complete, by extension, perfect. The definition continues:

Original Word: τέλειος, α, ον; Part of Speech: Adjective
Transliteration: Telios
Short Definition: perfect, full-grown
Definition: perfect, (a) complete in all its parts, (b) full grown, of full age, (c) especially of the completeness of Christian character.

Brought to its end, finished, wanting nothing necessary to completeness

Perfect, that which is perfect; consummate human integrity and virtue; of men; full grown, adult, of full age, mature

Dr. Ken Chant has defined, from all the above, that Telios means to be all we are at any given time. Thus, if we are eight years old, and acting as an eight year old, we are perfect, or mature, all we are to be. As God is God, we are who we are, in the one sense, in Christ, already perfect, complete, whole, and as people, we are to be mature, all we are supposed to be given our life experience, our training or education, and our knowledge of God.

It is important to remember it is God (see Philippians 2:13) who is invested in the process of our transformation, and it is also us (Romans 12:1-2 +) working on this important goal, of becoming all we already are in Christ.

It All Starts at the Cross

A brief summary of Romans 6:1-11 can help establish our identity, which is the place from which we can grow. Paul reminds us that:

We are baptized into Jesus' death, which affirms the reality of our New Birth, symbolized by our baptism in water, and further affirms that our sin nature, which stood in complete opposition to God has been done away with, our sin is forgiven, and our new life in Christ is begun…we are new creations in Christ, and can now begin to live as God intended, free from sin and free to choose life.

Also, Paul reminds us that were raised with Christ in resurrection, raised to a brand new life. Thus, the resurrection power of Christ lives in each of us, giving us the power to live life in victory…we are in him, he is in us, and we are eternally a part of the Trinitarian dance of love, Father, Son, Holy Spirit, and us!

Finally, we must affirm that we are seated with him in the heavenlies, at the right hand of the Father [Ephesians 2:6], far above principalities and powers, so we can rule and reign with him, now in the Spirit, and eventually to rule the New Heaven and Earth to come.

Again, in terms of our salvation and overall life in Christ, we can state categorically, as Jesus did on the cross, it is finished...and continues. Therefore...Now (Romans 8:1, 14) we do not live under condemnation, as those who have never experienced life in Christ, and we are truly children becoming sons... "For you did not receive the spirit of slavery to fall again into fear, but you have received the spirit of adoption as sons, by whom we cry, Abba, Father!"

We are not condemned, for we are all set free...from the law, the law of sin, and the law of death. Thus, Paul continuously affirms that we can rest in the finished work of Christ...his grace is enough and his work is done, and continues, thus are we...

Like a caterpillar to a butterfly, transformed into a new creation, old things (our old nature) is gone, and we are a new person on a brand new road of life. This is accomplished in us by the Spirit of God, the Holy Spirit, who is working in us to be all we were created to be. Of course, God is working in us, but we must...

Submit to his process of change, by daily showing up, presenting ourselves, as a living sacrifice, which is holy and acceptable, and makes very good sense.

Thus we must...

Respond, to the word of God and his subtle but continuous call to live according to our state, that is, as sanctified sons and daughters', knowing that we already have all blessings in Christ (Ephesians 1:3). Heaven is sure, and our life has purpose, not because of what we do or accomplish, but because we are a kingdom of priests. (Revelation 1:6) We do this...

By faith, we are to act according to what God has declared we are. We are men and women that have been bought with a price, that is, by the precious blood of Jesus, chosen, holy and loved (Colossians

3:12), and now fully able to utilize biblical principles and common sense to achieve our purpose in life.

How Do We Get Started?

I can hear many of my fellow strugglers, "if" transformation is our right, and virtually guaranteed because of Christ' finished work, how come I struggle so much? Well, transformation is simple…just not easy! It does require our participation to see that which was promised come into our reality.

Over many years of teaching and counseling, I have found the following scriptures, with brief commentary, to be especially helpful, but with caution. We must remember that we are not alone in our journey to wholeness or maturity…we have many tools available to us. We have the Word of God, the Holy Spirit, and the body of Christ…and the mind of Christ as a gift to us all. So, we begin with many advantages, and from a position of full and complete acceptance and love from the Father, through the Son, by the Spirit. With this in mind, here are a few thoughts on the process of transformation.

Paul reminds us in Ephesians 4: 17-24;

> "So this I say, and affirm together with the Lord, that you walk no longer just as the Gentiles also walk, in the futility of their mind, being darkened in their understanding, excluded from the life of God because of the ignorance that is in them, because of the hardness of their heart; (In essence, Paul would not have said not to do something that we could not do…so, backsliding if you will is possible, but not inevitable) stated and they, having become callous, have given themselves over to sensuality for the practice of every kind of impurity with greediness. But you did not learn Christ in this way, if indeed you have heard Him and have been taught in Him, just as truth is in Jesus, that, in reference to your former manner of life, you lay aside (get rid of, through down like an old coat that no longer fits) the old self, which is being corrupted in accordance

with the lusts of deceit, and that you be renewed in the spirit of your mind, (through the word of God) and put on the new self, (act what you are, a new creation, holy, loved, chosen) which in the likeness of God has been created in righteousness and holiness of the truth."

In my book, *Journey to Wholeness,*[1] I write extensively about this dynamic process...which is not a one-time event but an ongoing process as the Lord reveals to us areas of our lives which do not coincide with our new identity in Christ. Our journey begins with salvation, and continues towards our maturity. The desire of the Lord is to see all of us choose the path of difficult resistance, and put off the old, renew our minds, and put on the new.

To put off something means to first become aware of thoughts or beliefs that are contrary to God or common sense, and with a determined heart "throw it down", confess and renounce the lies we have believed, followed by renewing our mind through the word of God, then we are to put on, act out, by faith the opposite of the lie (truth), until the new becomes the natural norm.

The Brother of Jesus, James echoes Paul's statement above.

"This you know, my beloved brethren. But everyone must be quick to hear, slow to speak and slow to anger; for the anger of man does not achieve the righteousness of God. Therefore, putting aside all filthiness and all that remains of wickedness, in humility receive the word implanted, which is able to save your souls.

But prove yourselves doers of the word, and not merely hearers who delude themselves. For if anyone is a hearer of the word and not a doer, he is like a man who looks at his natural face in a mirror; for once he has looked at himself and gone away, he

[1] Journey to Wholeness: The Process of Growth and Change, Vision Publishing

has immediately forgotten what kind of person he was. But one who looks intently at the perfect law, the law of liberty, and abides by it, not having become a forgetful hearer but an effectual doer, this man will be blessed in what he does." (James 1:19-25)

Paul continues

"Therefore if you have been raised up with Christ, keep seeking the things above, where Christ is, seated at the right hand of God. Set your mind on the things above, not on the things that are on earth. For you have died and your life is hidden with Christ in God. When Christ, who is our life, is revealed, then you also will be revealed with Him in glory.

Therefore, consider the members of your earthly body as dead to immorality, impurity, passion, evil desire, and greed, which amounts to idolatry. For it is because of these things that the wrath of God will come upon the sons of disobedience, and in them you also once walked, when you were living in them. But now you also, put them all aside: anger, wrath, malice, slander, and abusive speech from your mouth. Do not lie to one another, since you laid aside the old self with its evil practices, and have put on the new self who is being renewed to a true knowledge according to the image of the One who created him—a renewal in which there is no distinction between Greek and Jew, circumcised and uncircumcised, barbarian, Scythian, slave and freeman, but Christ is all, and in all." (Colossians 3:1-11)

And the writer of the Hebrews states it this way.

"For the word of God is living and active and sharper than any two-edged sword, and piercing as far as the division of soul and spirit, of both joints and marrow, and able to judge the thoughts and intentions of the heart. And there is no creature hidden from His sight, but all things are open and laid bare to the eyes of Him with whom we have to do." (Hebrews 4:12-13)

"Therefore, since we have so great a cloud of witnesses surrounding us, let us also lay aside every encumbrance and the sin which so easily entangles us, and let us run with endurance the race that is set before us, fixing our eyes on Jesus, the author and perfecter of faith, who for the joy set before Him endured the cross, despising the shame, and has sat down at the right hand of the throne of God. For consider Him who has endured such hostility by sinners against Himself, so that you will not grow weary and lose heart. You have not yet resisted to the point of shedding blood in your striving against sin; and you have forgotten the exhortation which is addressed to you as sons,

"My son, do not regard lightly the discipline of the Lord, nor faint when you are reproved by him; for those whom the Lord loves he disciplines, and scourges every son whom he receives. It is for discipline that you endure; God deals with you as with sons; for what son is there whom his father does not discipline? But if you are without discipline, of which all have become partakers, then you are illegitimate children and not sons. Furthermore, we had earthly fathers to discipline us, and we respected them; shall we not much rather be subject to the Father of spirits, and live? For they disciplined us for a short time as seemed best to them, but He disciplines us for our good, so that we may share His holiness. All discipline for the moment seems not to be joyful, but sorrowful; yet to those who have been trained by them produces the peaceable fruit of righteousness who have been trained by it." (Hebrews 12:1-11)

All of these passages indicate the importance of our change.

Appling the word takes time, patience and perseverance. There is a process of transformation, which begins at the cross, and continues as a loving process of discipline, which is not punishment, but is focused on training and educating us to become fully what we were born to be…son's, inheritors…like father, like son.

A man ought to live so that everybody knows he is a Christian… and most of all, his family ought to know.

~ D.L. Moody, Evangelist

Chapter 3

Transformation:
Change My heart, change my wife, and change my life

Don't go changing to try and please me!

The song by Billy Joel is a catchy tune, but change will many times please us and others...and certainly will please the Lord (depending on the change of course). Remember, change is possible, but it takes time, and starts with a quick view of our reality; what do we need to change and how motivated are we to do it. Essentially, biblical change requires that we accept the truth of God's word, and recognize the areas of life we need to make changes in, affirming the reality of God's power to change us, as we cooperate with his word. Finally, we must trust the Lord to finish the work in us that he has begun, as promised in Philippians 1:6.

Remember, the work of our transformation, from God's viewpoint is complete, and continues...but we must follow the principles, best discussed in the previous chapter. An illustration of change can be seen in Paul's teaching often related to marriage and family life. Here are the key verses that help to bring us a deeper understanding.

> "Therefore be imitators of God, as beloved children; and walk in love, just as Christ also loved you and gave Himself up for us, an offering and a sacrifice to God as a fragrant aroma. and be subject to one another in the fear of Christ. Ephesians 5:1.

> Wives, be subject to your own husbands, as to the Lord. For the husband is the head of the wife, as Christ also is the head of the church, He Himself being the Savior of the body. But as the church is subject to Christ, so also the wives ought to be to their husbands in everything.

Husbands, love your wives, just as Christ also loved the church and gave Himself up for her, so that He might sanctify her, having cleansed her by the washing of water with the word, that He might present to Himself the church in all her glory, having no spot or wrinkle or any such thing; but that she would be holy and blameless. So husbands ought also to love their own wives as their own bodies. He who loves his own wife loves himself; for no one ever hated his own flesh, but nourishes and cherishes it, just as Christ also does the church, because we are members of His body. For this reason a man shall leave his father and mother and shall be joined to his wife, and the two shall become one flesh. This mystery is great; but I am speaking with reference to Christ and the church. Ephesians 5:21-32.

Keys to our change include:

Be an Imitator...but not of your father or mother, or a television family, or even of your spiritual leader (except as he or she follows Christ), but truly submit yourself to God and his word. This is progressive, that is, we are always, every day, working to give our lives to Christ as our Lord and King, and working to follow the example and teachings of Christ (love in action) in every part of our lives.

Mutual submission is also key...and it is wisdom to be open to submitting to one another as a higher submission than what is to follow. In other words, as a husband, I cannot demand submission, only slavery and that is not what the Lord wants for us. I expect my wife to be willing to submit to me in areas of my gifts, calling and purpose, and also expertise. Just because I am male does not mean I am good at all stereotypical male things, like mechanical work. If I am good at something, and the need for that gift avails itself, by all means my bride should get out of the way (submit) to my gift...but if I am not, and my wife is, then submission to her makes sense...it is not a gender issue, but one of mutual respect.

Love and Respect is required...between husband and wife, but of course, both need love, and both need respect, and our goal is to demonstrate love to one another in all things...thus, if we are submitted to be like Jesus, work to respect and submit to one another in all things, even esteeming each other as greater than ourselves. Then submission in marriage and all other relationships becomes easy, if not even comfortable.

Thus we must...

Respond in love, and accommodate one another, while at all times showing respect and affirming our differences, and steward the rest according to Biblical principles and common sense.

Leave and cleave is not leave it to Beaver

Genesis 1 then 2 speaks about the importance of giving up something to gain something better. In this case, it is essential to leave what has become comfortable, easy, to cleave (adhere to, become united with) what is not yet comfortable, easy, but is in fact a bit risky. Thus, in marriage, as in many other areas of life, leaving is key, and cleaving (total commitment) is essential but not necessarily natural. In order to be successful in the transition from its all about me to we, requires unselfishness, and the development of oneness, which does not imply sameness. In fact, we are blessed to have different personalities, different points of view. How boring life would be if we all thought exactly the same. Especially for a husband and wife. Developing the ability to let go of one's own selfish or even justified rightness to share life with another is necessary for success...we have to leave and cleave, with the goal of becoming one, requiring vulnerability and trust.

Genesis continues with the need to become truly open in relationship, naked, which is a similar word to revelation, but with the awareness that there is no shame in this relationship, as we have freely chosen to trust fully and love deeply, which is true freedom. Our covenant with each other, and with the Lord is freedom indeed, while recognizing that this vulnerability, trust, oneness, means we can be easily hurt by the very one we love the most. [see Genesis 3]

What about the Kids: Three Things

When my children were young I used to tell them "to obey is better than being sacrificed." Ok, it was a slight embellishment on the scripture, but my focus (until around age 12, when they were no longer children but emerging adults) was that obedience is key to getting along with me.

Children must learn to obey, but young people, from 12 on up, need to learn to submit willingly, so they can work towards the goal of maturity, or Telios. Of course, love and discipline is required, and we must remember, it is a marathon, not a sprint to maturity…and change, which though inevitable, is never easy.

Conclusion

Family life today is under significant attack by the media and other forces. Marriage has become almost throwaway, as defacto relationships have become more acceptable. In the Kingdom of God, a kingdom we have voluntarily enlisted in through our relationship with Christ, we have certain rights and privileges, and many responsibilities. For a husband to love his wife as Christ loves his church is not easy…and at time may seem nigh to impossible. But God gives grace. For a wife to respect and honor her husband might seem a ridiculous request and requirement from God, but God gives grace. And it takes grace to grow and change, and it is possible…for God does give grace enough for all.

The perfect church service would be one we were almost unaware of.

Our attention would have been on God.

– C.S. Lewis

Chapter 4

Transforming My Church

A couple of years ago I had the privilege of visiting what was touted as the Seven Churches of Asia Minor...the footsteps of Paul. The scenery was beautiful, and there are many historical things to see, but if you are actually looking for a church in Ephesus, or Smyrna or the rest, you will be deeply disappointed. They are not there.

The Turkey Trotter of churches of the Book of Revelation are no longer with us, which indicates that there is no guarantee our church will be here in the future. We know that Jesus is building his church, and the gates of hell cannot stop its progress, but our local congregation, in order to thrive and survive is the concern of this chapter. WE are to be the hands and feet of building his church, which produces key questions which I will attempt to answer here.

The first question is, what is the church? In brief, the church is made up of those who have been called out of the world (sin) and gathered together as a worshipping and governing community. Thus...

Who is the church? Well, it is made up of the whosoever will that come to Christ...but again, gathered with specific functions, such as preaching, worship, caring for the poor, healing, all under healthy leadership who helps the congregation serve in community.

Where is the church? The church of Jesus Christ is everywhere. Strong in some places, weak in other but always growing, for the church is alive and vibrant, and effective wherever two or three (or hopefully many more) gather in Jesus name.

The primary activities of the church can be described from the book of Acts 2:42-46, which states:

> "They were continually devoting themselves to the apostles' teaching and to fellowship, to the breaking of bread and to

prayer. Everyone kept feeling a sense of awe; and many wonders and signs were taking place through the apostles. And all those who had believed were together and had all things in common; and they began selling their property and possessions and were sharing them with all, as anyone might have need. Day by day continuing with one mind in the temple, and breaking bread from house to house, they were taking their meals together with gladness and sincerity of heart."

In summary, what we see here is the early church, which is our pattern, and was a church that emphasized:

The word of God, presented as apostolic doctrine, which is not doctrines per se, but foundational teaching on who Christ is, what he has done for us, and how we are to live our lives once we have received the wonderful grace of God.

Secondly, it was a prayerful and worshipful church, which appears to be more of a lifestyle than a service, as they daily worshipped and served one another, with incredible joy in their hearts. So, without a doubt it was a Family Church, as all things were in common or they were willing to share anything and everything they had, with open hearts and open hands with one another. Finally, they were...

A Generous Church, ready to share resources, unmotivated by manipulation, but fully motivated by mercy and grace, first to the family of God, and then to those not yet members of the faith.

The church (ekklesia) consists of all those who have embraced by faith Jesus Christ as Lord. To be the church requires more than one of course (where two or three are gathered) and consists of many functions. The primary activities of the church can be described from the book of Acts 2:42-46, which states:

"They were continually devoting themselves to the apostles' teaching and to fellowship, to the breaking of bread and to prayer. Everyone kept feeling a sense of awe; and many wonders and signs were taking place through the apostles. And all those who had believed were together and had all things in common; and they began selling their property and possessions and were sharing them with all, as anyone might have need. Day by day continuing with one mind in the temple, and breaking bread from house to house, they were taking their meals together with gladness and sincerity of heart."

In summary, what is seen here is the dynamic, functional early church, which is our pattern. It was a church that emphasized:

- The word of God, presented as apostolic doctrine, which is not doctrines per se, but foundational teaching on who Christ is, what he has done for us, and how we are to live our lives once we have received the wonderful grace of God.

- Secondly, it was a prayerful and worshipping church, which appears to be more of a lifestyle than a service, as they daily worshipped and served one another, with incredible joy in their hearts. So, without doubt it was...

- Family Church, as all things were in common, that is, they were willing to share anything and everything they had, with open hearts and open hands towards one another. Finally, they were...

- A Generous Church, ready to share resources, especially with the poor, unmotivated by manipulation, but fully motivated by mercy and grace, first to the family of God, and then to those not yet members of the faith.

Further, much can be learned, both positively and negatively, from reading Paul's many writings to various churches. I will only choose one for illustration; the church in Corinth.

The church in Corinth was a dynamic Church and no doubt an exciting place of worship. The gifts flowed freely (though out of control), Communion or the Eucharist was a true agape feast (though of control), in fact, pretty much everything they did was out of control. However, in the midst of the crazy of Corinth, some of the most important teaching is provided on what a local church, should feel like as representative of Christ in the earth.

This is described best in I Corinthians 14: 20-33.

> Brethren, do not be children in your thinking; yet in evil be infants, but in your thinking be mature. In the Law it is written, "By men of strange tongues and by the lips of strangers I will speak to this people, and even so they will not listen to Me," says the Lord. So then tongues are for a sign, not to those who believe but to unbelievers; but prophecy is for a sign, not to unbelievers but to those who believe.

> Therefore if the whole church assembles together and all speak in tongues, and ungifted men or unbelievers enter, will they not say that you are mad? But if all prophesy, and an unbeliever or an ungifted man enters, he is convicted by all, he is called to account by all; the secrets of his heart are disclosed; and so he will fall on his face and worship God, declaring that God is certainly among you.

> What is the outcome then, brethren? When you assemble, each one has a psalm, has a teaching, has a revelation, has a tongue, has an interpretation. Let all things be done for edification. If anyone speaks in a tongue, it should be by two or at the most three, and each in turn, and one must interpret; but if there is no interpreter, he must keep silent in the church; and let him speak to himself and to God.

> Let two or three prophets speak, and let the others pass judgment. But if a revelation is made to another who is seated, the first one must keep silent. For you can all prophesy one by one, so that all may learn and all may be exhorted; and the spirits of prophets are subject to prophets; for God is not a God of confusion but of peace, as in all the churches of the saints."

There is so much in this passage, but I will emphasize points for consideration.

- This church was one that "came together". Paul uses a word here for passionate expression between a man and a woman. It speaks of a commitment to bless, bring pleasure and satisfaction, creating greater connection or bonding. It required vulnerability, action not just contemplation, and its focus was the benefit of the other, not just the self. Often through this union fruit was born, expanding the family. We need to come together as congregations with anticipation and passion, for in doing so we produce...

- A prophetic presence which was experienced in the early church. So strong was the presence of Holy Spirit that people would fall under God's power and cry out "God is in the house"! It was from the powerful worship and purposeful preaching that presence (that is, the manifestation of his presence, as we know that God is ever present with us) was experienced and lives were transformed. Finally, there is...

- Participation, which was not from a platform, but was the responsibility of all members present. That does not mean everyone preached each Sunday, or had a prophetic word...but all, meaning all were encouraged to come to church with anticipation that the Lord could and would use them in service for God's glory. We need to have the same anticipation and preparation.

So, how can we reform our church? What will it take? But first, what's the problem...well, back to Corinth.

The Pauline Pattern and Purpose[2]

The foundation for the church was laid by the Apostles and Prophets (Ephesians 2:20) and is discussed first in 1 Corinthians 3:1-17. Because of the problems in this highly charismatic church, Paul was compelled to...

Withhold the greater revelation of God's purpose for the churches good, because of worldliness, which is to have the wrong values, including jealousy, amounting to covetousness, rooted in fear, quarrels over who had the better and more powerful father figure, stemming no doubt from insecurity and immaturity, leading to an ordinary rather than supernatural orientation towards life. The fact is, comparisons divide and conquer, for the Kingdom is to be team oriented, and those laboring in the kingdom as God's servants deserve wages owed, but the glory is God's. We must all remember God's house is his people, the buildings are secondary.

To build the House of God effectively, a foundation must be laid. Building the house of God requires a purposeful focus, therefore we must be careful how we build; his house is...

- A place where God's Spirit dwells

- Where the purposes of the Lord can be fulfilled

- Where God's people are nurtured and trained by confirmed leadership

Perhaps some brief reflections or pictures from the Word of God can assist our understanding.

The Purpose of God can be found in the beginning- (Genesis 1:26-28), with greater understanding revealed as we understand God's

---

[2] This portion is adapted from the book "Setting the House in Order", Vision Publishing

Government (Isaiah 9:6, 11:1-6, Revelation 7:9), which is to continue until God's glory is reveled in the earth, until the nations are either discipled or judged. (Habakkuk 2:14, Psalm 98:9)

Of course, Christ is our supreme pattern. Jesus called men unto Himself- (Mark 3:13), then taught them the ways of God (Matthew 5:1,2), through modeling the plan of the Father- (Luke 4:44, 18,19, John 12:27), with a purpose of preparing a team (Mark 6:7-13, Luke 10:1). Once released under the power of the Holy Spirit, this team would fulfill the purpose of establishing the Kingdom through the church (Matthew 28:16-28, Acts 1:6-8). Today, God is still working through his called and anointed leaders, starting with Five Fold ministry, Apostles, Prophets, Evangelists, Pastors and Teachers, along with Elders, Deacons and other ministries, all submitted to the leading of the Holy Spirit in a local assembly…at least hypothetically. For in truth…

It is always people that God builds with (Ephesians 2:1-22). These people are the dead now made alive; these are the people of God, formerly under the dominion of Satan, caught in lustful lifestyle, by nature children of wrath (Ephesians 4:25). But thank God. By grace we have been marvelously saved, in order that we might prove God's rich mercy, becoming his workmanship, demonstrating his grace and mercy by our good works as a general part of our lifestyles. As such we must remember…. Him!

Him Always in Him

It is helpful to always remember we were once separated from the Trinity but now are citizens, having become one new man in the earth; we are no longer aliens but fellow citizens with the saints, a part of the household of God himself. His ultimate purpose for us is to fit us all together as a growing, vibrant and alive holy temple of the Lord, a dwelling place for his spirit, together fulfilling the kind intentions of his will.

"Slowly, through all the universe the temple of God is being built. And whenever, in any place, a soul by free willed obedience, catches the fire of God's likeness, it is set into the growing walls, a living stone."

Phillips Brooks.

Chapter 5

Living Stones

I just returned home from two ministry trips, one to South Korea, one to a predominately African American church on the East Coast of the United States. In each venue, though so very different in style from one another, the passionate worship and dynamic fellowship of God's people was tangible. Being with them, I was reminded that as we worship together, style is not what matters, but changed hearts focused on praising and worshipping our wonderful Lord, and in doing so, becoming like vibrating stones which make up a portion of the wonderful and ever growing Body of Christ.

Peter writes in I Pet. 2: 1-10;

> "Therefore, putting aside all malice and all deceit and hypocrisy and envy and all slander, 2 like newborn babies, long for the pure milk of the word, so that by it you may grow in respect to salvation, 3 if you have tasted the kindness of the Lord. 4 And coming to Him as to a living stone which has been rejected by men, but is choice and precious in the sight of God, 5 you also, as living stones, are being built up as a spiritual house for a holy priesthood, to offer up spiritual sacrifices acceptable to God through Jesus Christ. 6 For this is contained in Scripture:
>
> > "Behold, I lay in Zion a choice stone, a precious corner stone, And he who believes in Him will not be disappointed."
>
> 7 This precious value, then, is for you who believe; but for those who disbelieve, "The stone which the builders rejected, This became the very corner stone,"8 and, "A stone of stumbling and a rock of offense";

For they stumble because they are disobedient to the word, and to this doom they were also appointed. 9 But you are a chosen race, a royal priesthood, a holy nation, a people for God's own possession, so that you may proclaim the excellency of Him who has called you out of darkness into His marvelous light; 10 for you once were not a people, but now you are the people of God; you had not received mercy, but now you have received mercy."

To summarize this simply, as believers we are:

- Believers in all the Word of God affirms regarding us; we are created in the image and likeness of God, chosen from the foundation of the world, bought with a price, redeemed from the curse of the law; when Christ died we died in him, when he was buried, we were buried in him (in type is our baptism in water), when he arose, we arose in Christ, and we have eternal life now. When he ascended, we ascended in him, and presently we are seated in the heavenlies with Christ. This is life in Christ. Thus, none of us were...

- Accidents, but were the Father's choice and precious to the Father, even in our sin, brokenness and shame. The Lord declares that we are...

- Holy; not becoming holy if we behave well enough (though in fact, there will be changes in our behavior because we are being conformed to his image daily) and thus we bring the sacrifice of praise for all he has done for us.

- Finally, we are not alone in all of this, for we are now a part of a new, chosen race, and not just miserable sinners hanging on to the mercy of God, hoping that someday the Lord will allow us into his presence by the skin of our teeth. We are a royal priesthood, Holy nation; and without doubt, peculiar... unique, different, fantastic in the Father's eyes...all provided

- By His mercy, grace and especially, his (agape) love.

Final Thoughts on the Church

There is much debate on the Church Universal versus the Church Local. Well, perhaps there is such a thing as a universal church made up of all believers in all times, but practically, what we have that is visible and tangible today is a local church, or churches in locality around the world. Our membership, though theoretically in the universal church, our body needs to be in a local church, where we worship, receive instruction, have fellowship and accountability, give and receive, under God ordained leadership. The option of not gathering together as a body of believers in a local church is not an option...but a privilege, and duty as we serve each other, the world and Christ.

The easiest entrance point into someone's life is a simple deed done in kindness.

–Steve Sjogren

Chapter 6

Transformation of the World

There are many metaphors used in scripture to describe the life of the church and believers in it. One that best befits our series is Peter's living stones. Having been brought to life in Christ, we have been made part of the very body of Christ, foundational to the purpose of God, for God to live with his creation in intimate fellowship.

This Sunday, when I start to fellowship, sing, break bread and share the word with my fellow believers, we will, as mentioned above, as living stones, begin to vibrate together in a symphony of praise to God. Whether the worship is charismatic or liturgical, our vibrations will be felt all the way to heaven. It is our joy to be a part of the temple of God.

The Kingdom of God is where we live as transformed and in process people of God. We have entered by faith (God chose us, and we said yes), and God calls us, woos us to embrace the way of a disciple, with determination to grow in grace, and conform ourselves to Christ' image.

To Transform a City

I am convinced that the Lord not only wants to transform us as individuals, in the family and in our churches, but also to transform the world through the church, until the Kingdoms of this world become the Kingdom of our Lord and Christ...and he shall reign forever. (Revelation 11:15).

The church can often become inward focused, more like a membership club than a vibrant fellowship of believers. The church is an instrument designed by God to see the integration of the good news and the good deeds of Jesus into the world. In order to do this, we must move from attractional or maintenance churches to Missional Churches. Jesus spoke of this in the following passages.

Matthew 22:2-5, Luke 14:18-20

> "The kingdom of heaven is like a king who prepared a wedding banquet for his son. He sent his servants to those who had been invited to the banquet to come but they refused to come. Then he sent out more servants and said, 'Tell those who have been invited that I have prepared my dinner: My oxen and fattened cattle have been butchered and everything is ready. Come to the wedding banquet. But they paid no attention and went off—one to his field, another to his business....and they all alike began to make excuses. The first said, 'I have just bought a field, and I must go and see it. Please excuse me.' Another said, 'I have just bought five yoke of oxen, and I'm on my way to try them out. Please excuse me.' Still another said, 'I just got married, so I can't come'".

> Then he said... Go out ...into the streets and alleys... Go out to the roads and country lanes...so that my house will be full."

Good News and Good Deeds are to work together, expressed in the culture in which we live (some would say the 7 Mountains of Culture; business, government, media, arts and entertainment, education, the family and religion).

Jesus' Ministry

> "You know the message God sent to the people of Israel, telling the good news of peace through Jesus Christ...how God anointed Jesus...with the Holy Spirit and power, and how he went around doing good... because God was with him." Acts 10:36-38

Good deeds create good will which opens the door to good news. In Jesus ministry people were "amazed," "astonished," "marveled," "wondered," etc. When we go about doing good, nearly 100% of the time you will be asked, "Who are you?" "Why are you doing this?"

Of course, this opens the door to dialog about Christ. In fact, when the church responds around the world to crisis, helps build hospitals, develops orphanages, etc., people will be skeptical.

But remember, Peter stated,

> "Who is going to harm you if you are eager to do good?" 1 Peter 3:13-15

Good deeds alone are not Good News in itself. People, left to their own will intuitively arrive at the wrong conclusion:

> "Amazed and perplexed, they asked one another, 'What does this mean?', 'They have had too much wine." Acts 2:12 "Why do you stare at us as if by our own power or godliness we had made this man walk?" Acts 3:12 "We are only men, human like you..." Acts 14:8-18

Of course, we know that personal faith is necessary, for..."Faith comes from hearing..." Romans 10:17

Though this is true, deeds alone are not enough, but deeds verify the words...words clarify the meaning of deeds. Thus, we need both good news and good deeds. Transformation is the result of both compassionate deeds and passionate proclamation of the gospel.

"The social gospel divorced from personal salvation is like a body without a soul; the message of personal salvation without a social dimension is like a soul without a body. The former is a corpse, the latter is a ghost." E. Stanley Jones.

It's About the Kingdom of God

Unfortunately, we often settle for conversion rather than transformation." Our call is to take the gospel to the whole world, expanding the Kingdom of God. This was a major theme of desire when Christ came, and was his primary message, Peter and Paul's primary concern, and the only real message of John the Baptist.

"In those days John the Baptist came preaching in the Desert of Judea and saying, 'Repent, for the kingdom of heaven is near.'…People went out to him from Jerusalem and all Judea and the whole region of the Jordan. Confessing their sins, they were baptized by him in the Jordan River." Matthew 3:1-5

We must think "Kingdom" if we are going to see the heart of God fully manifested in the earth, the Father's world, our world.

We Must Think "Kingdom"

The birth of Jesus announced that the King had come, and thus his Kingdom would soon be established.

- Isaiah 9:6,7— "For unto us a child is born…and he will reign on David's throne over his kingdom," the angel

- Gabriel—Luke 1:31-33 "He will be great…and will reign…his kingdom will never end"

- The Magi—Matthew 2:1, 2 "Where is he who was born king of the Jews?"

- Simeon—Luke 2:25 "…he was waiting for the consolation of Israel."

- Anna—Luke 2:38 "…she spoke about the child to all who were looking forward to the redemption of Jerusalem."

- Joseph of Arimathea— "waiting for the kingdom of God" (Luke 23:53, Mark 15:43).

So Again, We Must Think "Kingdom"

For it is central to the message of the gospel:

- First public words of John and Jesus—Matthew 3:2, 4:17

- First petition—Matthew 6:10

- First priority—Matthew 6:33

- Message of his disciples—Matthew 10:7

- Post resurrection message—Acts 1:3

- Phillip—Acts 8:12

- Paul's message—Acts 17:7, 19:8,9, 20:25 28:23,31 (Paul preaches Kingdom 16 times)

- Bookend passages of Acts (Acts 1:3 & 28:31)

What is the Kingdom?

I have covered this topic more fully in my book, *That's the Kingdom of God,* but here is a brief summary for consideration.

The kingdom of God is any place over which God has dominion. A view of the benefits of Kingdom life are found in many scriptures, but most profoundly in Isaiah 65.

- Physical / Spiritual Aspects of the Kingdom--Isaiah 65:17-25…and in the Kingdom…

- There is joy—v.19

- There is absence of weeping and crying (v.19)

- There is no infant mortality (v.20)

- People live out their full lives (v.20)

- People will build houses and live in them (v.21, 22)

- People will sow and reap (v.21, 22)

- There is fulfilling work (v.22)

- There is confidence that their children will face a better life (v.23)

- People will experience the blessing of God (v.23)

- People will have intergenerational family support (v.23)

- There will be rapid answers to prayer (v.24)

- There will be an absence of violence (v.25)

Of course, when Christ came, he did so not just in word, but in demonstration of power. This helps us understand the miracles of Jesus…again, summarizing.

> Matthew 11:4-5 "Are you the one who was to come?" Jesus replied, "Go back and report what you hear and see: The blind receive sight, the lame walk, those who have leprosy are cured, the deaf hear, the dead are raised, and the good news is preached to the poor."

Jesus miracles were called "signs" of the kingdom—attractive glimpses of what the kingdom will be; fast-forward to the future:

- Because children don't die in the kingdom…

- Because there is no premature death in the kingdom…

- Because there are no hungry in the kingdom…

- Because there are no deaf, blind, lame, etc. in the kingdom…

- Because the kingdom is a place of inclusion…

Some would say, "isn't this the American Dream, or Australian, or?" It may be a dream, but the reality is that no individual nation, no matter how noble, will ever fully embody the values and provide the benefits the Kingdom of God does.

So, we see that the Kingdom benefits are provided, but primarily because of the values of the Kingdom as discussed in the Sermon on the Mount…where we see:

- Children are valued and held in high esteem—Matthew 18:2, 19:4, Mark 10:14

- The poor are blessed—Luke 6:20, James 2:5

- Those persecuted for righteousness are blessed—Matthew 10:9

- Servanthood is valued over power--Matthew 20:21ff

- We love our enemies, do good to those who hate us, bless those who curse us and pray for those who mistreat us (Luke 6:27,28)

- It's a life where marriage is honored (Matthew 5:27-35)

- It's a life of reconciliation (Matthew 5:21-26)

- It's a life of good deeds (Matthew 5:16)

Kingdom work involves a variety of people—believers and unbelievers:

- Matthew 13:47-50 "…all kinds of fish…"

- Matthew 13:24-29 "…let them both grow together…"

Of course we enter the Kingdom through the new birth, which allows us to see the kingdom that we were blind to prior to Christ. This is presented in John 3:3-5.

Jesus builds the church and the church helps build the kingdom, the embodiment of what life looks like when living under the reign of God—an attractive and compelling alternative to "what is".

Everyone senses that things are not the way they are "supposed to be." As believers and potential leaders, we must somehow explain to the world the greatness of our God, their need for him and the benefits to be obtained in the Kingdom.

For we know that:

- People are separated from God

- Self-awareness / Self-centeredness reigns supreme in our culture, which leads to

- Conflict between people (war, hate, racism, etc.) and even the

- Exploitation of the planet (global warming, etc.)

But there is hope...change is possible, full and complete transformation...but we must take seriously what Paul declares in 2 Corinthians 5:17-21.

> Therefore, if anyone is in Christ, he is a new creature; the old things passed away; behold, new things have come. Now all these things are from God, who reconciled us to Himself through Christ and gave us the ministry of reconciliation, namely, that God was in Christ reconciling the world to Himself, not counting their trespasses against them, and He has committed to us the word of reconciliation.

> "Therefore, we are ambassadors for Christ, as though God were making an appeal through us; we beg you on behalf of Christ, be reconciled to God. He made Him who knew no sin to be sin on our behalf, so that we might become the righteousness of God in Him."

Transformation means reconciliation...starting with being reconciled to God through Christ, which was done for us, unilaterally, covenantally, and permanently by Jesus for us on the cross...dying as us, we now are reconciled, as him. It continues to our families, and ultimately through the local church to the whole world. God has called each of us, in our own small way to be ambassadors of reconciliation, loving, forgiving, and serving the King in his kingdom. He has given us grace to be transformers in the world, and grace to change in the ways we must in order to become the transforming agents he desires.

www.ingramcontent.com/pod-product-compliance
Lightning Source LLC
Chambersburg PA
CBHW060058050426
42448CB00011B/2522